MR. WHITTIER
AND
OTHER POEMS

Books by W. T. Scott

———

To Marry Strangers
The Sword on the Table
Wind the Clock
Biography for Traman

Mr. Whittier

and Other Poems

BY

WINFIELD TOWNLEY SCOTT

New York

THE MACMILLAN COMPANY
1948

TO

Esther Willard Bates

Acknowledgment

The author thanks the editors of the following
periodicals for permission to reprint many of the
poems in this book: The Atlantic Monthly,
Contemporary Poetry, Poetry, and the University
of Kansas City Review. "Hamlet and Hamlet" was
read before the Phi Beta Kappa chapter
at Brown University on
March 13, 1947.

Contents

I

Mr. Whittier

It is so much easier to forget than to have been Mr. Whittier.
Though of course no one now remembers him when he was young.
A few old ladies who were little girls next door in Amesbury,
Or practically next door, have reminiscences of pears and apples
Given them by the famous, tamed, white-bearded saint with the
Still inextinguishable dark Hebraic eyes; and
Of course there is the old man—and I for one am grateful—who
Recalls the seedy coat, the occasionally not so clean high collar,
And that like many another he read his paper by the hour in the privy.
Carl Schurz, finding him rained in by the stove at the village store,
Thought 'So superior to those about him, and yet so like them;' and
His official biographer decided that Mr. Whittier's poetry was the
       kind
'Written first of all for the neighbors.' There are lesser and worse.

In any case, here is a city, founded in 1630, present population some-
       where about
55,000—has been more in boom times, and has been a lot less;—say,
In three hundred years has birthed a couple of hundred thousand
       people
And one poet. Not bad. And as proof of the title I shall only remark
It is easier to leave *Snow-Bound* and a dozen other items in or out of
The school curriculum than it is to have written them. Try it and see.

Born where the east wind brought the smell of the ocean from Plum
       Island up-River,
At a brookside haunted in the foggy dark of autumn nights
By six little witches in sky-blue capes—Uncle Moses had seen
       them;—

3

Born on a farm to the *Bible, Pilgrim's Progress,* a weekly paper, the
    Quaker meeting-house,
To hard poverty, obscure, and a few winters of country school;
To die—though only after there were thirteen for dinner, and the clock
Suddenly stopped—ancient with fame, with honorary degrees, and
One hundred thousand dollars all made out of poems—I say
Even this was not easy, though also it is not
What I am talking about, but is really incidental along with
Not liking Walt Whitman and never quite affording marriage.

Neither, under the circumstances, could it have been easy, and it
    was important,
To stand suddenly struck with wonder of old legends in a young land,
To look up at last and see poetry driving a buckboard around the bend,
And poetry all the time in the jays screeching at the cats in the door-
    yard,
Climbing with the thrush into the August noon out of the boy's sight
As he dawdled barefoot through poetry among the welts of the
    goldenrod;
But nothing is hardest which treads on nobody else's toes.

Let us not begrudge Mr. Whittier his white beard, his saintliness,
    his other foibles;
Let us remember him when he was young, not to begrudge his rise
As a goddam Abolitionist hated not only in the South,
Hated by manufacturers, politicians, his neighbors, our folk, all
Who hate the outspoken radical and know a safer way;
Denounced by the clergy—a serious matter in that time; by the good
    men who
Rotten-egged him in New Hampshire, burned him out in Pennsyl-
    vania,
Jailed those who read him, and twenty years later immortally froze
With Webster on whom he turned his scorn of compromise.
It is so much easier to forget than to have been Mr. Whittier.

He put the names of our places into his poems and he honored us with
    himself;
And is for us but not altogether, because larger than us.
When he was an old man, the Negroes came to him free to come and
    sang to him
'The Lord bless thee and keep thee;
The Lord make his face to shine upon thee and be gracious unto thee;
The Lord lift up his countenance upon thee, and give thee peace.'
—No more begrudge their freedom than his tears.

'After Great Pain
a Formal Feeling Comes'
(Emily Dickinson)

What is rejected becomes a greater thing.
All things referred draw drama from its size.
So Amherst can become the fabulous sun,
One yard a kingdom and one house a castle,
One room a throne, and dry within that room
One closet be the casket of a name.

Call Emily. And fetch a mischievous dance
Of petals and butterflies and bees turned stars
Turned fireflies between the hedge and window
Where the girl in the white dress glimmers and goes.
Offstage, the larger terror than we want
Save in the larger eyes of those returned.

But there's a dance—a ballet of Emily:
A thousand of her in pirouetting white
Like great revolving daisies all the way
From her father's door over into the graveyard—
A gay haunting in the middle of town.
Then as in a movie this dissolves.

Speak to the stone and to the grass and to the door:
Where is Emily? The Sabbath noon
Is still and empty, or is only still,
Or is not even quite exactly still.
By such singleness is singularity
Made multiple, and Emily everywhere.

She knows now the necessity to deny
The Father, Son, but never the Holy Ghost.
She weds the Holy Ghost and it is death—
A going down under the garden beds
And then a resurrection as if alone;
The mountain of darkness taken into her.

Only through denial great acceptance
As only in depths of silence the tall song:
She walks here as immortal as the light—
Made indistinguishable from the air,
Having the self-possession of the sun.
Emily is Emily is Emily forever.

Wilson

We walked with him in the rain, road after road,
But each time we came to the place we were alone,
We would not go in; and we turned alone with the words.

Abandoned far behind us the room was a ruin
Of tumbled desks, spilt books, and faded maps;
Only the schoolmaster's voice sternly repeating
Repeating whatever we still had strength to hear.
We turned and turned beneath words and could never hide.
But when we followed and came to the place we would not go in.

We returned to the bright and easy fields of the country;
For thunderous hours the shadows of planes passed over us
Multitudinous crosses. Then in the hollowed silence
The voice began again repeating the words and the place.

His was the only conspicuous defeat, the only defeat of importance.
Our enemies' defeat and our victory were the same.
They believed in the body's resurrection as performance of the wor-
    shiped body,
What had failed should be made larger, the goldener calf.

When at last we came to the place he could not go in;
He who came down from the mountain with the law
Yet led us on past the shattered slates, knowing the pieces
No more than his broken body—receptacle merely:
Henceforth the words informed and survived in our flesh,
Woke and arose in the bodies of our enemies, or did not live;
Knowing the teacher is never the ultimate participant,
The wage of his vision is death, is not to cross over.

8

We walked with him in the rain, road after road.
Would the breaking of his body be sufficient
If through crack of the bones the quickened spirit
Struck sun broad upon land that lay ahead?
The voice repeated, repeated that this was the way.
When we came at last to the place he was there before us.

May 1506
Christopher Columbus speaking:

I do not want your praises later on.
When I am dead I shall rest easier
In lack of borrowed breathing; and you will
Be tempted—never doubt—to sweeten up
Your own names with the fame of praising mine.
Even your scoffing mouths that so reviled me
Can learn again the shape of knew-him-when
And claim a talking share in India.

I began beggar and I finish beggared—
Beggared of gold and trumpets and renown
That Spain one moment lent me. It is nothing.
The unpaid tavern bill, the leaking roof
I would bequeath to later dangerous men
As their insurance of a happy death.

Feed on my bones if that will make you fat,
I can't prevent your feast; but all that marrow
Shall not fetch you memory of those beaches
And how they glittered beyond the tired sails.
Beggared I am but never of that look.
O rebels, traitors, slanderers, embezzlers
Who stole and lied to get me rags and chains!
I had my strength, but yours was cleverness;
Yet mine that troubles you the most, the longest.

God forgive me. Christ save the King and Queen
To whom I freely will all India.
I was no longer young when I first voyaged
And I was old and gutted at the last.

How did I harm you? Was my fame my crime?
Did my light, coruscant light of a new land
That was to shine for all, diminish yours?
Or did you think a feeding claw could hold it—
The gold—this side the King and the Word of God?
In that great wake beneath the foreign stars
What little Caesars sailed the charted course
And swarmed like eager spiders on the treasure
As though they could not wait to make it ruin—
That I had looked upon to name and bless.

Viceroy of India, Admiral of the Seas.
I wrap my names about me like old flags
That have had honor once, as well you know.
My grave has room for them and truth and me.
Cape Gracios à Dios and Veragua,
Andalusia's long way to Española,
Farthest-followed sun and under it
The curve of surf falling forward west.
Why did you hate my finding India?

Job Townsend and John Goddard

I pray Job Townsend and John Goddard:
Why you ancestral spirits have not shared
Your cleverness of hands, and I secured
That ceremonious perfection
Of praising and glorifying wood—
Its jointure a miracle understood
In matched discoveries the chisel bared
All locked together and so made
A new way for mahogany to have grown:
Taught me to summon by inheritance
The scalloped seashell curving deep within
The burnished bole fragant from the forest,
And I one bed or—better yet—one desk
Brought to closer tolerance.

Unwatched, habitual gesture all at once
I watch: my hands caressive over briar
Open pouch, fill pipe, fold pouch, set fire
Tobacco—my practised fingers evidence
An independent skill so intelligent
I become learned in all they have learnt
Of an efficient and organic grace,
Required unselfconsciously acquired.
If this continual chore of mine could do
So much to me—then what those all-but-sired
Blocks and slabs of resinous wood to you?

I pray again: may my most inward desire
That would invent whole forests and bequeath

This land dark tracts of legendary trees—
As though not you but I were ancestor—
Know that neither the body nor the spirit
Can such wonder-working ways inherit;
Each man in his own flesh begets again
A new collaboration with the sun;
God's hand is shaped by what it worked upon.

Gert Swasey

Have you ever asked yourselves—ladies, ladies—
    what it must have been like
To have been Gert Swasey?
To have a rich father,
To run away from home
To be a circus queen, and
To come back a charlady?
To come home and be old?
Dirty and old?

Few of you now can remember Gert Swasey
When she was young—how she was young:
What was it like do you suppose
To drive through town as though you thumbed your nose,
Your red hair flying, and beautiful clothes?
What was it like to want to do that
Seventy years ago—ladies, ladies?
Gert was a wild one, and when she wanted
She'd drive a pair of horses like a witch enchanted.
She'd drive them down from Mount Washington
As though she were fired out of a cannon;
And all the way along Merrimac,
Up Main, through Summer street, down Mill and back
Till she charged up the driveway of her father's mansion,
Twice around where the iron stag stared,
Then as fast to the coach-house as she dared
Which was twice as fast as anybody dared;
The horses snorting and all in lather,
But there was nothing Gert would rather

14

Than set the whole downtown awhirl
Gasping at that Swasey girl.

I wonder how it was to be that Swasey girl
Not a Sanders nor a Dow nor a Saltonstall,
But new-rich Irish with no family at all
Save a sporting father who kept a stable.
It must have been both mad and sweet
To thunder through leaf-filled Summer street
Disturbing the ladies at the tea table,
Disturbing the ladies in the summer house,
And all along Merrimac's shops and factories
The men's quick faces.

Then to run away—to run far away
To ride in a circus—
The colored wheels
The tights and spangles
The lights, the crowd
The wonderful horses,
The plumed, proud, wonderful white horses,
The tremendous music.
To travel like a gypsy
To dress like a queen
To see all the world that she'd never seen
That was never the world where she had been.
Not a Dow nor a Sanders nor a Saltonstall
Unless they paid to get in.
And then
After thirty-five years to come home again.

Have you ever asked yourselves what it must have been like
To be the old charlady at the B. & M. railroad station?
To clean the toilets

To mop the floors
To be greasy and gray
To be poor and alone
To be Gert Swasey?
Then there is a way—easy to learn—
Of talking to yourself,
Answering yourself,
When there is no one else
Wherever you are.
There are many stray cats, a dozen—fifty—
That will stay in your house
If you will feed them,
Lock them in to keep them safe,
Whose yowling some day wakes the neighborhood
But, at last, not you.

Have you ever asked yourselves what it must have been like
To have been Gert Swasey?
To be a rich young nobody with red restless hair?
To run away from home
To be a circus queen, and
To come back,
And to be old, and to be dirty, and to be dead—
O, ladies, ladies.

16

Winslow Homer

Fog. He can see only this deep still fog.
Roweled by the falling sun it smoulders westward awhile
But it closes impenetrable curtains: night is fleshed.
No shore, save for the long jut of staggered rock
Shelving a black sharp stair to the burdened, hidden sea.
This he paints in his old age, recording his utter love.
For him there is one canvas, thick with seventy years—
Picture over picture buried, each worked from the last.
Where are the children's faces in the morning schoolroom?
Far under battlefields of the Civil War,
Eaten out by tenser light, man-riddled noon.
Even summer landscape empty kept a memory of people—
Visitors passing and strange. Then one seaman storm-struck.
All vanished now, washed over in a high tide of paint
As though the colors of the world, faster and faster whirling,
Spun this still center of gray; this inevitable mist:
Sun lost, sea filled and covered,
The great stair of black rock deserted, used no more.

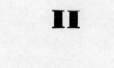

Hamlet and Hamlet

Elsinore: A Platform before the Castle.
Midnight.   Two Ghosts:

HAMLET

Though I am dead, oh I am haunted still.
Mortmain—mortmain: upon me even now?
Does that same hand which pulled me toward my grave
Yet drag me out of it for further death?

KING

I am your father, Hamlet. Were I sane
Being both your begetter and your slayer?

HAMLET

How should I know, who will not have a son.
Yours may have been a madness kept for kings—
That, too, I'll never know. And then again
It may be general between here and hell
If one has left a hostage in his name
To work it out. Who's marked for murder now
That, though the dirt is not dry over me
And no stone tells the place among so many
All newly dug, you call me back again
Against the midnight and the westward star?
Is any left to kill? I learned the dead
Can kill: but not each other.

KING

                                             Hamlet,
As far as death is kindlier than life
I'd hoped to find the dead forgive the dead.

21

HAMLET

Odd words from you. I take them for a father's.

KING

Listen, my son: wind rises and far down
The sea is thrashing higher, for the world
Turns toward the steeper east. The brightening stars
Flash inward their corroborative sign
That they have little time. And you and I
Are left with what they have before the cock
Cries up the light that washes us away—
Our quarreling white shadows both dissolved
Into the sun's decision. We shall die.
Wholly and rest if we can find our peace.
Can we not pause for that and then forever?

HAMLET

I see a sort of peace around us here:
Dark—dark and all but toppling with the dead
Who did not ask for this. My wretched uncle
Who killed you for the power and the Queen
And got them and drew all this after them—
Whose blessing did he have before your curse?
Why was he let? And wasn't that enough?
See how revenge upon him caught us all—
Pompous Polonius and, son for son,
Laertes and myself—and from that poison
Another potion for the Queen; and from
My feigning madness real for Ophelia.
All dead and gone. Inside these walls which gleam
And shudder in the imperturbable light
Of those unstaying stars, all strangers now.
All strange. All ruin. All silence. Is that peace?

KING

So ends the world.

HAMLET

               Was it thus ordained?
Tell me: were you privy to God's book?
Did you foresee the slaughter, now return
For one last look upon it and to bless it?
Ah, did you—tell me! —did you will my death?

KING

O Hamlet, Hamlet! Evil that struck me down,
Evil that emerged from the same womb
Which dropped me, forming me a righteous man,
Had seized the realm in which you were beloved,
Entered the very body of your mother.
It was as though a part of my own blood
Blackened with infection yet could be
Knifed out and spare the whole to heaven again.

HAMLET

And in the cutting what a wound was made!
That large it bled a kingdom.

KING

                      At my death
You mourned me with such passion of despair,
More even than is dutiful in sons,
I thought you were in love with death itself
And courting it.

HAMLET

               Yes, so I almost won.
I lost a father but I was no father.
I got a father who could not be mine:
So lost my mother. Then I gained a ghost.

KING

But if I gloved my dead hand within yours—
As though a virtuous Abel might avenge

23

Through his regeneration murderous Cain
By a reversal on him of his act,—
I thought as much to move the death in you
Outward against its source and cleanse you of it.
Alas, the sword is colored by its thrust.

HAMLET

Whom did I move against? I never knew.
Whenever I put my hand upon the hilt
It weighed as though I hefted up my heart.
And when I drew at last upon Laertes
Who crossed me as the slayer of his father
I might have been his uncle, or my own.
Who was I then? Where could I find myself?

KING

That was the burden which you would not bear.
I had forgot how slim a boy you were
When, right or wrong, I married you to murder.
My death that should have manned you in my place
Made you a gelding with a memory
Hot, confused, by turns afraid and vile.

HAMLET

Ah, you accuse me still!

KING

Some fault was mine.
Death does not cloak us in a wise man's magic,
But in these days while dissolution wears
Slowly upon us until we are gone—
As even now we two await the sun
Which soon all air will breathe to filling flame—
We watch awhile. Perhaps in recollection
Of others or ourselves we stay awhile
Gazing upon it all. Not wholly judge.

24

As if the phosphorent flesh itself remember
Though but an iridescent failing vapor
The shape of hand, the murmur of the pulse.
For we are never utterly purified
Out of that flesh till we are gone too far
To know or care, even to recall our names.
Interval of intelligence remains
Between the midnight and the foreign morning
That lights another history on the earth
In which we are a scattered, nameless dust.
Interval of the echoing of love
Possible only in the living body,
In us withdrawing homeward to the sun.
We are its lingering music. Mine the sin
That in this over-lengthened interval,
Made powerful by my willing and your wanting,
I sought to heat this to a vengeful brand
And marked you wickedly.

HAMLET

                        Oh, Father! Father!
Why was I not smothered in your death?
Half-breathing, half-awake; why was I left
A dreaming paralytic—too afraid
To follow and too dispossessed to stay?

KING

There was the halfway that you tried to take,
Like a tall dancer spinning mad between
Earth and sky in alternate aversion.
All believed but you and so you failed.

HAMLET

Laertes played my braver self. I thought:
If his blade overpower mine, it's mine.

25

We fused from common cause a common end,
And where we fell lay double suicide.

KING

And who was Prince that day?

HAMLET

Why, there was none
Because there was no king in Elsinore.

KING

My brother Claudius was king enough.
All had their death before he suffered his.
Polonius—

HAMLET

I speared him in the dark,
Thinking him greater fish.

KING

Perhaps. Ophelia—

HAMLET

Never my wish! All my desire! O death,
Grave magician of zeroes out of zero!

KING

The Queen—

HAMLET

Another's accident.

KING

Laertes—

HAMLET

Most deliberate and least intentioned.
My own scratch opened first.

KING

                    And then the King!
What a mound of carcase you bestrode
Before you stood up tall enough to reach
Into his heart! And then the thrust that got him
Seemed your arm's involuntary twitch.
Dying, you touched him cold.

HAMLET

                    My lord forgets
The last news that I had: my mother's death,
The poison on my sword. And then I stood.
And then I was alone. And then I moved.

KING

Revenge. My son, it took so long a route
That when it came I wonder whose it was?

HAMLET

Stones rolling down a mountainside: the one
Knocking against the next—so on—till all
Dispersed they lie and quiet at the foot,
With no more morals than the mountainside;
And none can tell the first stone from the last.
Cleaner the mountain stands, but who's to say
How much, or what the difference is in that?
Oh, I am getting weary for my grave.
I would be carried like a little boy
And put to bed again; for I am tired
Of all the toys of death. Where is the morning
That is my night? The starlight worries me
As though the world had stopped and heaven were fixed,
Trigged here forever with us—and no story
Save one, and none to tell it but myself;
It sickens me and will not make me sleep.
I'm cold.

27

KING

       Translucent pictures of my arms
That once when stout for pleasure of the task
Sometimes when you were small did nurse's work;
So warm a weight your head against my shoulder
I would delay upon the corridor
Or carry you the long way to your room,
Wishing I knew a song.

HAMLET

                   I don't remember.
Look! Does the east show there a milky line?

KING

It spills a little I think that side the sea.
The cock will spy it first. Trust him to warn
The world into its flesh again and blast us
Out of our tranced adventure. Peter heard it
Twice before he knew how cold was truth.

HAMLET

I wish I might have Peter's knowledge now.

KING

Never, until after Peter's sorrow;
And then no man can tell you truth from tears.

HAMLET

Then I betrayed you? Speak!

KING

                 You are not Peter.
Had you betrayed yourself—then me also.
But self-deception you could not contrive.
In desperate reasoning to be free you tried.
And yet you could not.

28

HAMLET

I cast this way and that.
As though I tossed in chains. It was the vow.
You swore me to swear vengeance on your death
And then the death was hung on me like iron.
I rattled with it every step I took.
I stopped and waited—then would step again—
This way and that—not quite believing it
Unless I moved— and then all frigid horror.
Everywhere there was no one but I.
And everywhere I could not find myself.
A ring of mirrors of my own invention—
I wheeled among them searching for a door.

KING

I think no exit gave except this one.
We walk tonight across that shattered glass
Hearing the crunch and tinkle of those deaths
As though some pretty instrument were smashed
Which once made music; now beneath our feet
Glint scattered, dimmer than most distant stars,
But with the question if they had to be.

HAMLET

I said your ghost was Satan up from hell
Arrayed in father's guise to purchase me.
Then proved it false.

KING

Almost against your hope.

HAMLET

Had you been King of hell and not of Denmark
I'd been relieved of murder. I had grief
Enough to weigh me down.

KING

                      When I returned
I was a king of moonlight armed with shade,
The cold reflection of the day. O night
That trembles now at pressure of this dawn
Bring back once more my scepter, make me king
Of anything—of waves, winds, rocks, myself,
Of Hamlet even!

HAMLET

                  Your name and mine are one.

KING

My shadow fought to lodge within your flesh—
Assume your blood and bone, inhabit you
With my avenging ghost, take on your warmth,
To be another Hamlet, be my son.

HAMLET

To make me King and father, yet myself?
Then who was Prince and who was in his court?
What thing upon the throne? Whose Queen in bed?
Who was beloved Ophelia if not Queen?
How was the Queen another but my mother?
What scarred Ophelia then? How could I love?
How could I kill? Oh, I inherited
A scrambled madness of incestuous nightmare
In which the faces interchanged—the play
Went wildly round and round before a throne
On which there sat a king as heretofore,
Who still embraced my mother and who grinned
Like a conspiratorial daddy, winking
To bid me share the gaiety, put off
The black reminder I had had a father,
Or I had been a son. Who was I then?
Who was I if not Hamlet, Prince of Denmark,

Nor Hamlet, King of Denmark? Was I both?
Then damned and double damned to work it out—
The live avenger and the dead betrayed:
Joined confusions and impossible
Yet joined indeed.

KING

My son, forgive my hands
That are a scattering smoke, blown mist through which
Even paler starlight shines to show
How emptied of all human heat they are,
Being no longer useful to take others'
Or touch a head or beat upon the air
Because what most they loved has now become
As thin a ghost as they, and by their guilt.
Since now in death we are in fact as one,
In these last moments listen to me, Hamlet,
And grant it stay the memory of my voice
As you have loved it best, if you can love
Even my name, which is your name, again.

HAMLET

I hear you still.

KING

In life we are as one
But not undifferentiated death.
I sought to enter the forbidden way.
I strove to make you proxy of my seed
But not to sow a life. I should have known
That witling Claudius my surviving self—
I, shorn of all but lust for Queen and power,
Dead-ended, that was I upon the throne,
And death was there and would have been enough.
If anyone was Satan it was he—

Not up from hell but fallen out of heaven
With his ambition round him like a net
Certain to choke him. All my sins upon him
Save sharp resentment of accomplishment
That should have seen his victory too rotted
Long to sustain its hour. But forth I drove you
As my begotten son to teach revenge.
And it was that you wrestled to betray.
I staked my death in you. You fought. The death
Was never yours until the end. I see
Your life was mine but only if it lived.
Out of mine but broken off—not leashed
For an incredulous continuance.
My more would be your less—your less my loss—
And thus it was. See now what I have done!

HAMLET

Ah! but it's over save the sound of it
Upon Horatio's tongue and a few more
Who will report these things and fix the blame
A dozen ways by Sunday and forget
By Monday. We are through with all of that.
Evil will call up evil on itself
Without the intercession of the dead,
And our tried remedy of self-destruction
Will not be questioned—old authorities
Are all with you and me. Laertes, dying,
Taught me my text as I outwaited him—
He gave me his forgiveness and took mine
Which now I understand and would bestow
On my beloved father; which to give
Is most to have and keep. And, oh, this peace
In my own name upon us all.

32

KING

— The cock!
Hear how he kindles on the day's new hearth.

HAMLET

Fade, Father! And so I! Leave light to earth.

Definition

This habit of avoiding unpleasantness: it avoids
Poetry, it avoids love; which is to say it brings
Dissimilarities together without revelation;
It is a sodomy; it chooses, in the long run, war.

It bears both a lily and a gun; an idiot, it
Crazes all conversation in its neighborhood and falsifies
The air we breathe. Indeed, it is against air. It distrusts
The sun. To worship death, to endure itself, it invents God.

The Ivory Bed

Who has not beheld fair Venus in her pride
Of nakedness, all alabaster white,
In Ivory bed, strait laid by Mars his side,
And hath not been enchanted by the sight?
                                        —GEORGE PEELE

The treading pigeon arcs his wings
As though his love were sped with flight,
And muscular with morning flings
The slated sunrise out of night.

Below him in the public square
The sailor, soldier, and marine
Get up and go away to war
From copulation on the Green.

Strange girls get up and go away.
In grass beneath the General—
Immortal bronze assured on clay—
Death's flat and rubber fingers fall.

That generation drains to grass
Without the twenty years' delay
In which to learn for what it was.
So peace begins the winsome day.

Pvt. John Hogg

In the war—oh, not the last war nor the one before—this was
Eighty-odd years ago and nobody now—the Civil War—

I can see—the way it still—beyond the white picket fence the little
    white farmhouse and the door
Open to June sun—the terrible way the young man left—leaped out
Between the rusted lilac and the yellow roses and ran up the road.

Did his wife with the baby girl, the boy clutched at her apron, follow
    to the dooryard?
I think so—but of course now nobody—though I am sure his father
    sat alone in the house;
And his mother—this is what I was told—what I know—lay across
    the doorsill: why he leaped that way that day.
Because she had said over and over 'Don't—don't—don't' and
'If you go it will be over my body.'

Wind running the sun in the trees and the short beat of his running
    up the summer road and gone,
Oh, it is so long ago and now there's nobody saw him and nobody
    sees him but me; and there's nothing.
It was all for nothing—running through the sweet dust to his death
    in a fevered bed off New Orleans harbor.
Nobody has anything now of his except some blood.

Three American Women and
A German Bayonet

Outweighing all, heavy out of the souvenir bundle
The German bayonet: grooved steel socketed in its worn wood handle,
Its detached and threatening silence.
Its gun-body lost, the great knife wrested to a personal particular
    violence—
Now bared shamelessly for what it is, here exposed on the American
    kitchen table and circled with the wreath
Of his three women, the hard tool of death.

And while Mary his mother says 'I do not like it. Put it down'
Mary the young sister, her eyes gleaming and round,
Giddily giggles as, the awkward toy in her left hand,
She makes impertinent pushes toward his wife who stands
Tolerant of child's play, waiting for her to be done.
His mother says 'I wish he had not got it. It is wicked-looking. I
    tell you: Put it down!'
His wife says 'All right, Mary: let me have it—it is mine.'
Saucily pouting, primly frowning
The sister clangs bayonet on table; walks out
And her mother follows.

Like a live thing in not-to-be-trusted stillness,
Like a kind of engine so foreign and self-possessed
As to chill her momently between worship and terror
It lies there waiting alone in the room with her,
Oddly familiar without ever losing strangeness.
Slowly she moves along it a tentative finger

As though to measure and remember its massive, potent length:
Death-deep, tall as life,
For here prized from the enemy, wrenched away captive, his danger-
   ous escape and hers.
Mary his wife
Lifts it heavy and wonderful in her hands and with triumphant tender-
   ness.

Forgive Me, Stranger

Shrive me? Can it be Tuesday now?
Can I be touched, washed, blessed, made whole?
Stayed so on Wednesday? Sir, I fear
Who touches me feels acid; so beware.
And I am cold, sir, also; bitter cold.
You cannot come near if I say you can't,
And you are not the child I put aside;
How can you touch me? In this garden
Are rocks and sand with roses, and beyond it
Spit and nails and vinegar and nothing.
Can you drink night? That gravel pit of stars,
They'd cut and choke you. Better, vinegar
Or even nails and spit; best of all, nothing.
Or could you if my thought believed you could?
No, I will not eat this blackness for you,
For I am cold enough. Go shrive yourself,
And I will lay one hand upon the other
To find if doubled zero makes warm wealth,
Or swallowing my tears turns salt to wine.
I'd heard the child was here who'd comfort me,
Having some wisdom about sleep and singing
Which I've forgot; but you are old and strange,
And no more help to me than I to you.
Forgive me, stranger; and—I'll—oh! my hands!

Day of the Russets

The boy, the man, and the old man in the orchard
Gathered russet apples all day long.

Their feet printed frosty grass of the morning,
Boy's running, man's steady, grandfather's scuff.

The little grove, fragrant with ripened russets,
Took them in just as it took the sun.

Grandfather picked what he reached, father on ladder;
The boy filled burlap from the brown-green ground.

There were big fall-defying bees, I remember,
And grackles that kept sorting the field.

Too fast at first for talk, too tired later,
They worked, and also too much at ease.

Afternoon resumed sound of small punches
Apple by apple now not quite so cold.

But the day grayed with the sun southwest,
Northeast the dull clouds beginning to shut.

The boy quit, to start eating the harvest,
Sitting half asleep except chill hands.

Toward the last, grandfather went picking flowers,
Coming back loaded with asters in the dusk.

My Grandmother Townley's Funeral

The slow procession of old people begins now
Enters now the fragrant room and crossing
Bends with the weight of its own emptiness
And makes a moving scythe toward the open coffin.

Garnering nothing it turns upon itself,
It moves in a measure of pauses, a hesitant
Numbed and ordained last dance, a shuffled grief
Circles like a withering wreath before the dead.

Like understudies of a retiring star,
Shyly they look and leave her where she lies,
And each returns to himself and goes out alone.
In the vacant room the flowers begin to dry.

Late Summer

Alder-side by water fringe, Oriental
With cat-o'-nine-tails, soothed with pads, all
Quick with red-wings, deft with spiders,
Not deep nor dim but drowsed; far with firs.
Clear. Cool. And beyond moss gentle beyond
Fronds of goldenrod, late summer weighted: pond.
Flicker of fish, silver dart over bronze treasure,
Lost and beautiful, abandoned, emptied cans, or
Roots' dark, octopus-vengeful; all image-doubled.
The plains of August august, autumn-troubled.

Seven Lines

Crisscross of hawthorn bush in snow.
Spill of tacks—a thicket—snarled barbed wire: no:
Thorn bush under low ceiling, thrust
Out against wind-troughs of snow-crust:
Unwalked, birdless acres, the air stiff and
Sun gone gray. This diamonded, transfigured dust.
Thorn-thicket: tallest, last thing in this land.

Identities

We cut the grass open,
We dug out the coffin,
We lifted its cover.
After years—nearly twenty—
We let the sun on her.
She lay as we knew her—
In the dress we remembered
And the face of her sleeping—
One moment, then perished.

It lay flat as a portrait
Old, dim beneath cobwebs.

For another's convenience
We caused her removal;
We looked to confirm it—
No mean, ghoulish motive.
But thus did we lose her.
We watched the air smash her,
Her fall from our loving,
Escape from our memory.

O, our multiple errors—
That the dead need move over
To placate the new dead;
That one not of our time
Would sustain introduction;
That we could assume it
And not be changed coldly,
Hurt too by the sunlight.

Puzzled and lonesome
We fitted grass over
The new grave and left her
Who, leaving us twice, had
Just now left forever.
It was she had confirmed our
Identifications.

Now That Lost April

Now that lost April returns with the sky
The roads are all dizzied with puddles awry,
The pastures in surf where the bluets are sown;
O the warning my mother would make to me once:
Put something over you when you lie down.

No matter how stilled stands the summery air
The thin threads of east wind shudder somewhere,
Deep in hot daisies cool smell of the ground;
O the warning my mother would make to me once:
Don't fall asleep without some cover on.

Though autumn is slumbrous in umber and high
The forests break open at weight of the sky,
The leaves shred the blood-red, the dry-shaken brown;
O the warning my mother would make to me once:
Have something over you when you lie down.

So in all seasons all lovers beware
Of the cold drill of darkness which spins in the air,
The whisper of spring saying *Winter has come*—
Of the warning my mother would make to me once:
Keep cover over you—keep cover over you—
Keep cover over you when you lie down.

Sixteen Lines

Let fall your gold again
O gold-green maple flowers
Crisscross the morning hours
With your nostalgic rain
Of sun-excited showers
Let fall your gold again
Until the pouring air
Drift gold-green everywhere
The sidewalks all along
In all your gold again
Your living carpet wear
Breathe out such sweetness there
Might yet again be song
Peace memory meaningful pain
O gold-green maple flowers
Let fall your gold again

Blue Fish in a Blue Sky

Blue tissue on slat sticks, the kite
Angrily rattles, argues with air,
Springs tensely near overhead in bare
Naked March, in scudding light

As the plunging boy downhill strings
It farther out. It wrestles the wind.
At level peril airways thinned
As water loosed of ice, it rides—it swings

Up in sudden surety—sloughed amateur
Awkward—glides perfect incline.
Now it is a blue fish on his line
Running far in the wind, in its pure

Element high charging, changed, till
Twitch of taut string balks a flight.
Kite sways a-leash at slim height
Above tiny boy braced on the little hill.

He plays-in his beautiful blue fish.
Hooked hard, it bucks stretched cord,
Loops over, rolls wild where it soared,
Diving as though to headlong finish

Leaps side to side. Held it spins
Then streaks down to treacherous trees'
Coral sargasso tangle. But he's
Edging it inch by inch, and wins.

Now clear and close and tamed and tossed
It shudders then slaps flat aground;
Sticks, blue tissue, lifeline wound.
Possessed as meant: almost but not quite lost.

Aria Major

As music well remembered in the mind—
The aria major spiralling secret dusk—
Yet falters on the insufficient voice:
So speak not this, speak not this love.

Wing after wing the fans of evening open
Arching across the sky till massed they stretch
Silent the perfoliated night:
So speak not this, speak not this love.

Wherever underneath midnight you lie,
No longer near enough for me to keep
And soon no longer small enough to hold:
This love, this love, this love I cannot speak.

Fifteen Lines

Song sparrow makes a joyful noise
Unto whatever Lord there is
Or, for all of that, to none.
In unpraised flights of praise
Above the pond the swallows play,
They dance a wreathing water and sky,
The choreographers of May.
Honor fitting for this day
Like me they could not know, but they
Are its honor. As a human
In a time of major wars
And minor verse
I would rehearse
Their practice sessions in the sun,
Their encores ignorant of applause.

North Light

Strict invisible wedge untaken,
Immortal interval whose slow increase
Moves with millennial patience;
Dark core in light, shadow of noon
Which defeating us lights us now:
North light: my windows that have no
Sunrise or set save by reflection;
Snow-light; leaf-light; outward, earnest
With chimneys, angled with roof-slant,
Nostalgic with skylights, and slate-stitched.
To island shingle infrequent Crusoes
Climb and repair but never stay:
Invasions unheld, foreignness too great.

North light inward: painters' nonpartisan
X-ray. Here skeletons walk
Being understood, and each thing flames—
Roses, scissors, books and table—
In generation its own sun,
Its joy self-held and emanated,
Its victory shared: individual, whole.
So, too, full-length in mirrors
Stone-naked, 35, the man
Alone between marriages,
Lustrous body entirely stilled.

My desire is for this light only
And long as it may be borne, thereafter
As often; and I know this light is

In me and the room together:
When I am not here the light is not.
Though I stand and stark mirrored
I am abased in its cold pride.
It is earned and given, both; and I
Have made first payments and got
An interest of knowledge, certain now
I work in playgrounds—so this light
May at midnight harden to a star.

A and B and the Mirror

You there—I here—triangled with the mirror
So it is just your face I see, you mine.
Neither turns to the other, nearer. It is clearer
This way, and at once your eyes begin to shine

And you smile, and I, in quick understood sign
That this is somehow funny and somehow charming,
At first for a moment alarming, then disarming
Not least because it happened without design.

Neither of us speaks—as though this were a magic
Occurrence in whose accustomed logic this un-
Accustomed transference had been done:
Travel has winked and desert plunged pelagic,

And above all we are alone together,
By our shared depth of common light seen clear
Till we laugh for terror, turn and wonder whether
To dare strength to do it again: I there, you here.

Communication Established

Asleep in the night I dreamed that you owed me a letter,
Over and over I dreamed that you owed me a letter.
But when I awoke in the daylight then I remembered
It was other way round, the other way round.

Well, when I was adolescent—in misery mature—
I would dote on the years to come when all must be sure.
Now I see how the green years are greened by their dreams
     of the future—
All the other way round, other way round.

In my art in my century only the old men try singing—
Bare Venus buckled to gray-bearded Mars and clinging.
Those of us yet a-quiver at thigh stand talking
All the way round and around.

I have therefore traveled, my love, to live in our living,
Over and over one green year the time we are living.
For the lechery of lyrics and letters is not lost in loving—
O the other way round.

'We Are So Fond of One Another, Because Our Ailments Are the Same'

There are no girls among us now with small high breasts,
No hard-thighed youth—no man of us golden now.
We have come to this middle island. We are here together.

Across other surfs in seeming other suns we can see them—
The quick-limbed, the nimbus-haired in their reckless and useless
    racing
Bright along the tide edge. If wise we watch without desire.

For we are nakeder than they, in our imperfections, in our being
    together,
Friends and lovers so long, coming through so many waters, so many
Signs exchanged and discarded, and sharing a few graves and our
    fearful love of children.

To this ripe and middle island, the sun stronger and sweeter since
    we know
How swiftly it can go out. We make love deep and slowly afternoons
In the sea sound. We glance back now without bitterness or envy.

Our hands so long have known the shape of each other in the day
    and night,
Change interchangeable, voices and silences easy, solitudes shared.
You nearest—how more than ever tenderly endearing the gray in
    your hair.

Tenants of the House

Beyond this house a rock-jut interrupts
The curve of field: right angle rock shoulder
Sharp and sudden, gray out of the grass:
Incunabulum of skeleton.
Then pond; then pine; and farther west more fields
Crowding a burdock-burdened family graveyard
Rickety slated, faint with fading names.

But there has been no death in this young house.
All earlier houses gone, we live alone
On hungry land in this unseasoned house,
That gray rock a bared bone-thrust of earth,
The slates remindful and the fingering sun.

And now whose dust and bones are those? Can we
Inherit, purchase, hire such ancient death?
But none is alien, uncontinuous
Though names are signed at last by someone else
And only strangers write them into stone.
We live alone but with the coming child.
That night I dug him, oh I dug his grave.

Memorabilia

Dottle of pipe ash drops dry through the pond water
And the brown pond water sifts it gray down and gone;
Water surface shifts, clears, and shows—amidst haloes of alder
Fresh-leafing in May sun—my face, heavy heavy stone.

The phoebe weeps in the woods and the robin chuckles.
Smell of the sun rises out of grass and the rotting bridge;
Beyond me the long sound of falling water. The sky twitches
Small clouds and over my face money-bugs, spiders, midges

Crawl, skate by the dangerous edge. And so I come
To my thirty-seventh season of spring counting so many rings,
Deliberate follies and accidents of wisdom and without fame
Less local than lilacs; though for this rural moment not minding

My face carved out of water, for the real stillness and imagined peace.
Not satisfaction. Not contentment. Only the insomniac ambition
Sliding dry through the air as last year's oak leaves
Incidental to mulch. Repeated business of spring is resurrection,

Not distance but renewal, leaf for leaf's sake, new growth green
In its own place by the pond side, twelvemonth repeating its variety.
Days consume the years but the May day is the waking-dream,
What the morning says to do, the light between the water and the
      sky.

Between one life begotten and one to come, both mine, I have come
To this end of winter wish to be taller than I am. Identity is all.
I watch the spiders at my work, spinning the current as they can.
I stand up and walk through the woods and go home to my love.